I Am a Little Pastry Chef

Mayumi Oono

We need some tools to bake:

Flour sifter

Cookie cutters

Whisk

Bowl

Scale

Measuring cup

Measuring spoons

Timer

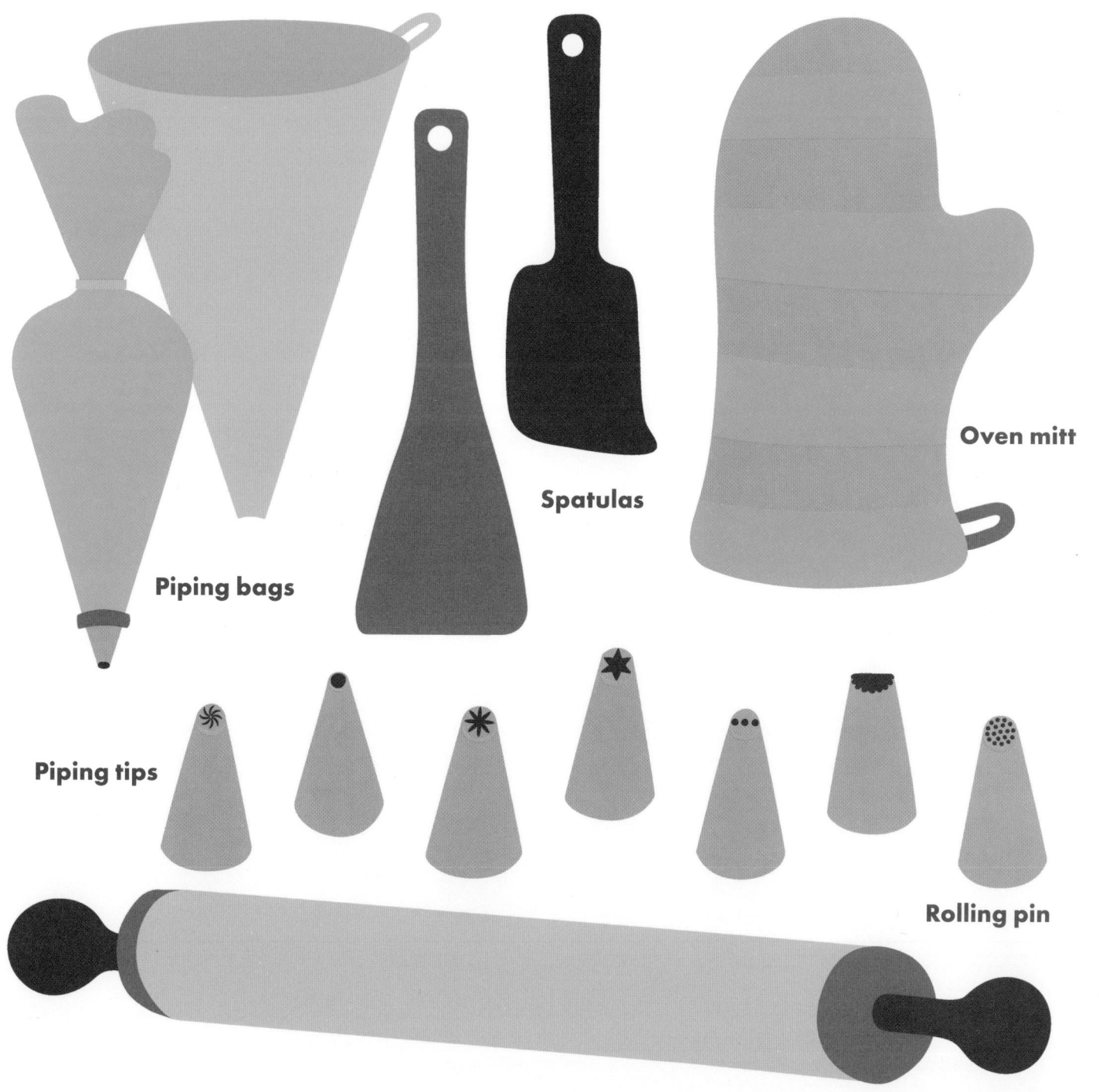

Piping bags

Spatulas

Oven mitt

Piping tips

Rolling pin

What should we bake today? First, choose a dessert...

Currant cake

Chocolate-raspberry cake

Doughnuts

Cupcakes

Chocolate lava cake

Macarons

Cookies

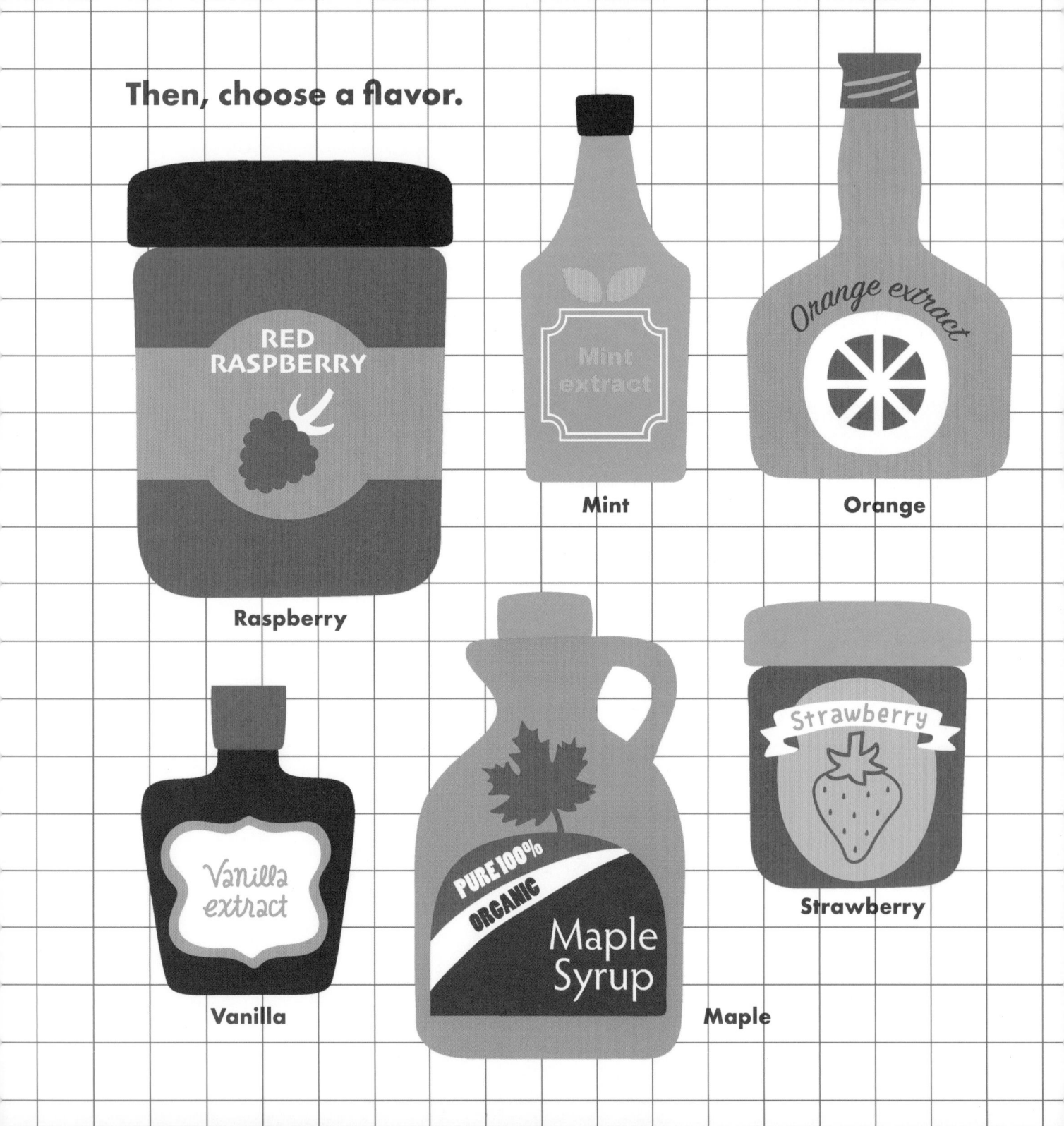

Then, choose a flavor.

Raspberry

Mint

Orange

Vanilla

Maple

Strawberry

To bake a cake, you need to mix the ingredients.

This is the fun part—cutting the dough with cookie cutters!

If you want to bake muffins,
it's time to fill the muffin tins.

Complete your creations with delicious decorations!

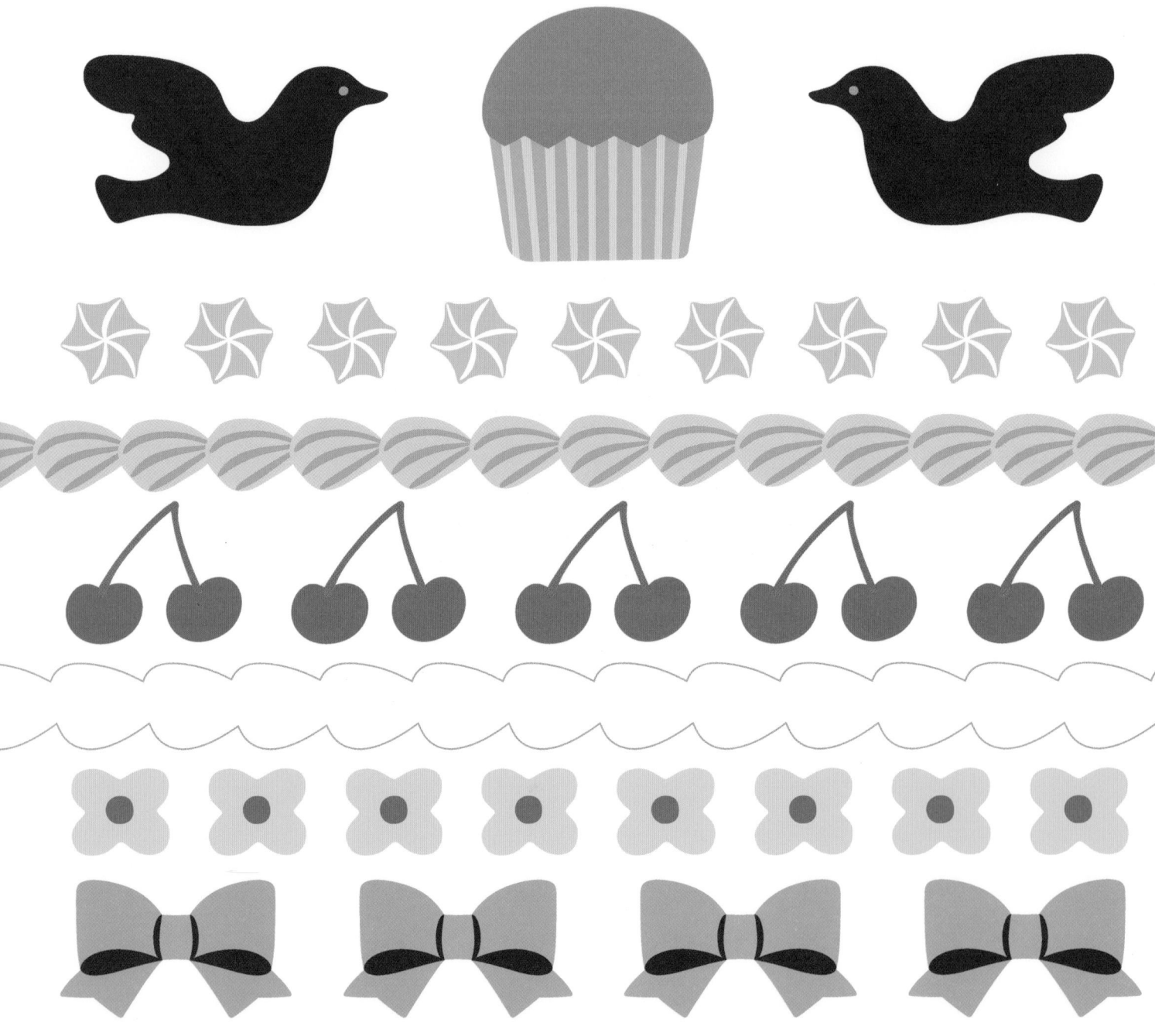

Decorate the frosting on these cupcakes.

Add some frosting...

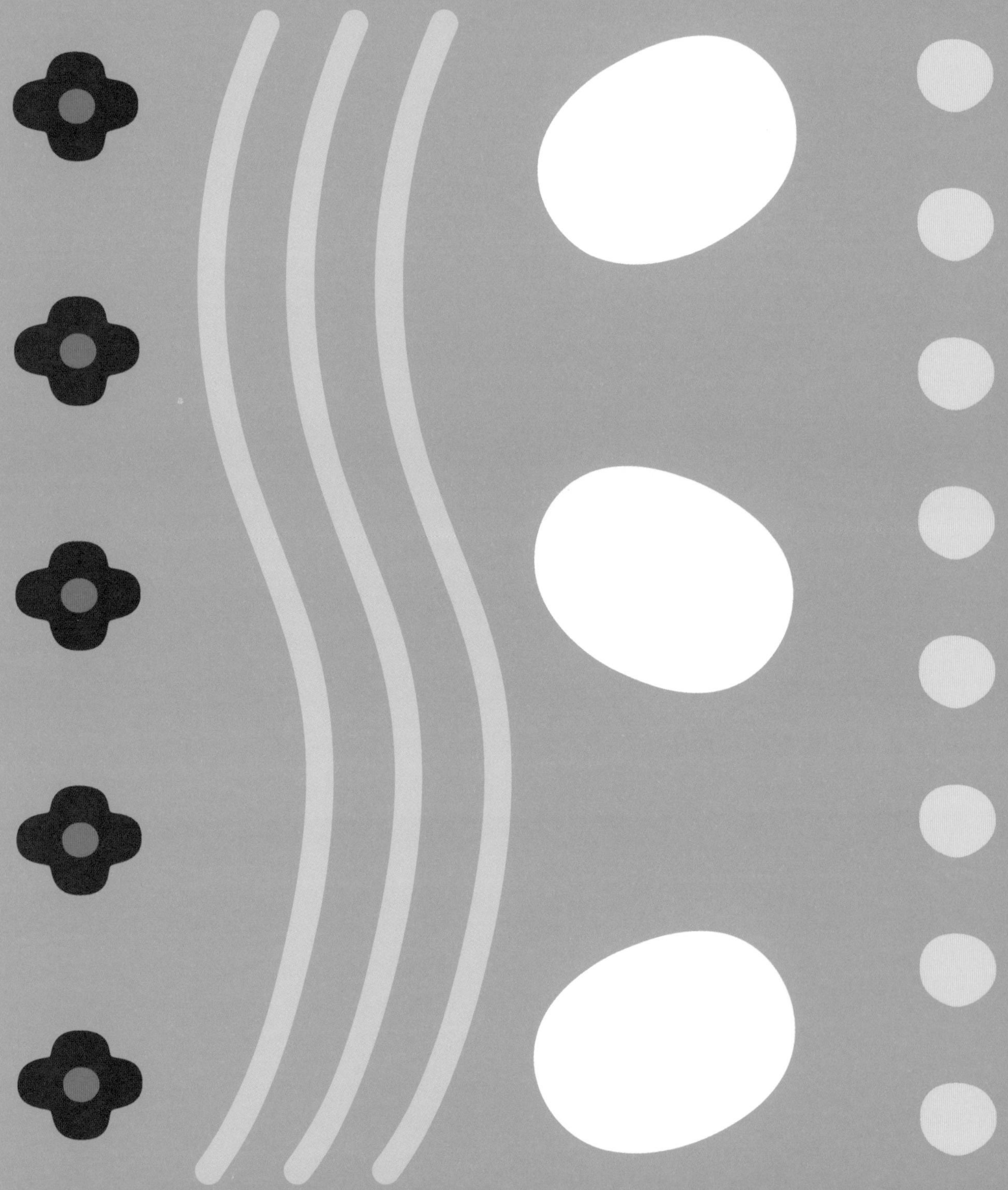

Decorate these cookies with frosting!

Decorate these desserts!

Decorate the doughnuts!

Decorate the cakes!

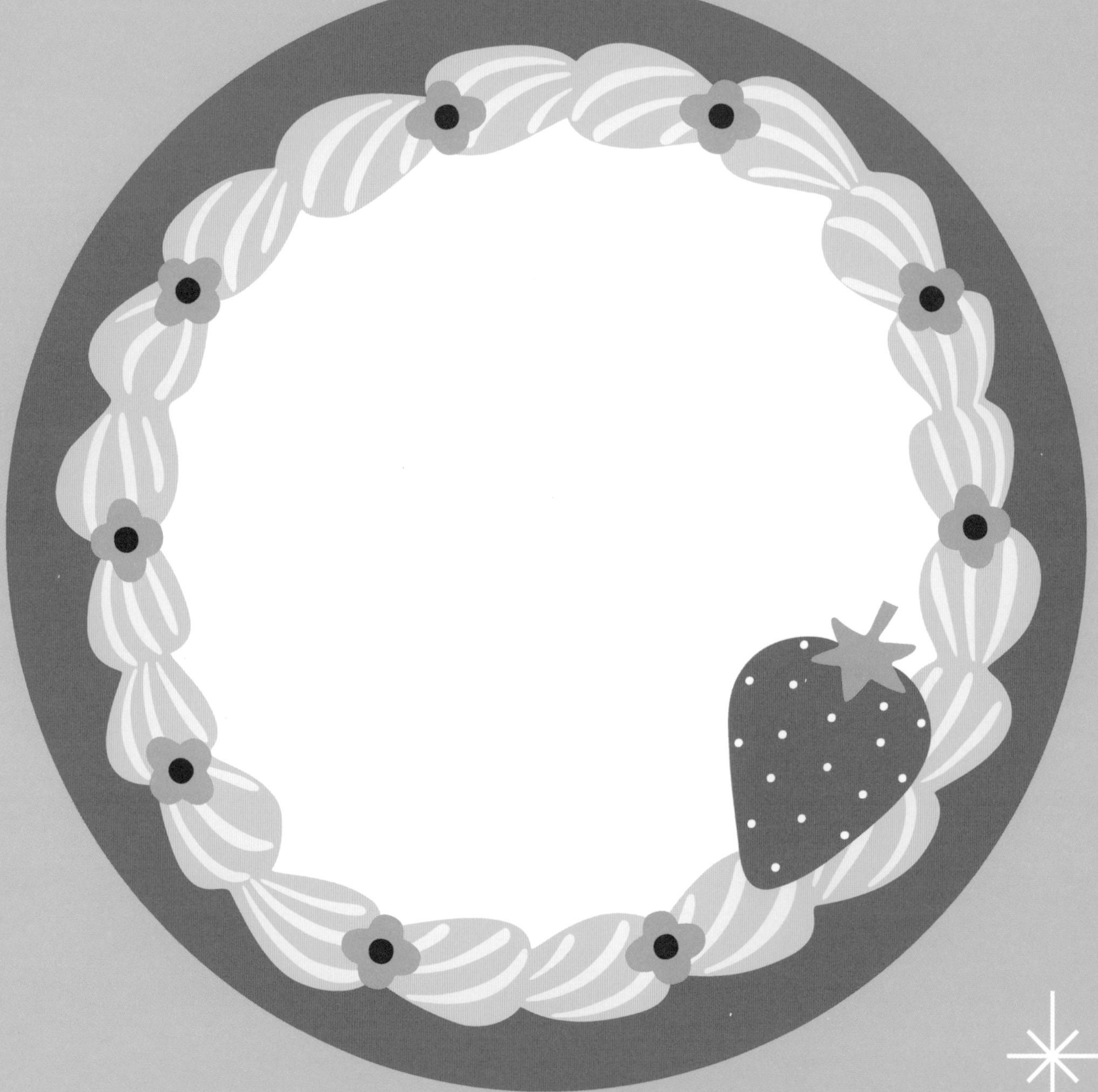

Special thanks to Mika Ogawa (Micarina).—MO

Little Professionals: I Am a Little Pastry Chef first published
in the United States by Tra Publishing 2022

Text, illustrations, and paper engineering © 2021 Mayumi Oono
Original edition © 2021 Zahorí Books, Barcelona (Spain)
Original title: *La meva petita pastisseria*

Printed and bound in China
ISBN: 978-1-7347618-4-9

Little Professionals: I Am a Little Pastry Chef is printed on Forest Stewardship
Council certified paper from well-managed forests.
Tra Publishing is committed to sustainability in its materials and practices.

MIX
Paper from
responsible sources
FSC® C102842

Tra Publishing
245 NE 37th Street
Miami, FL 33137
trapublishing.com

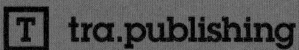 tra.publishing

Now do it yourself!

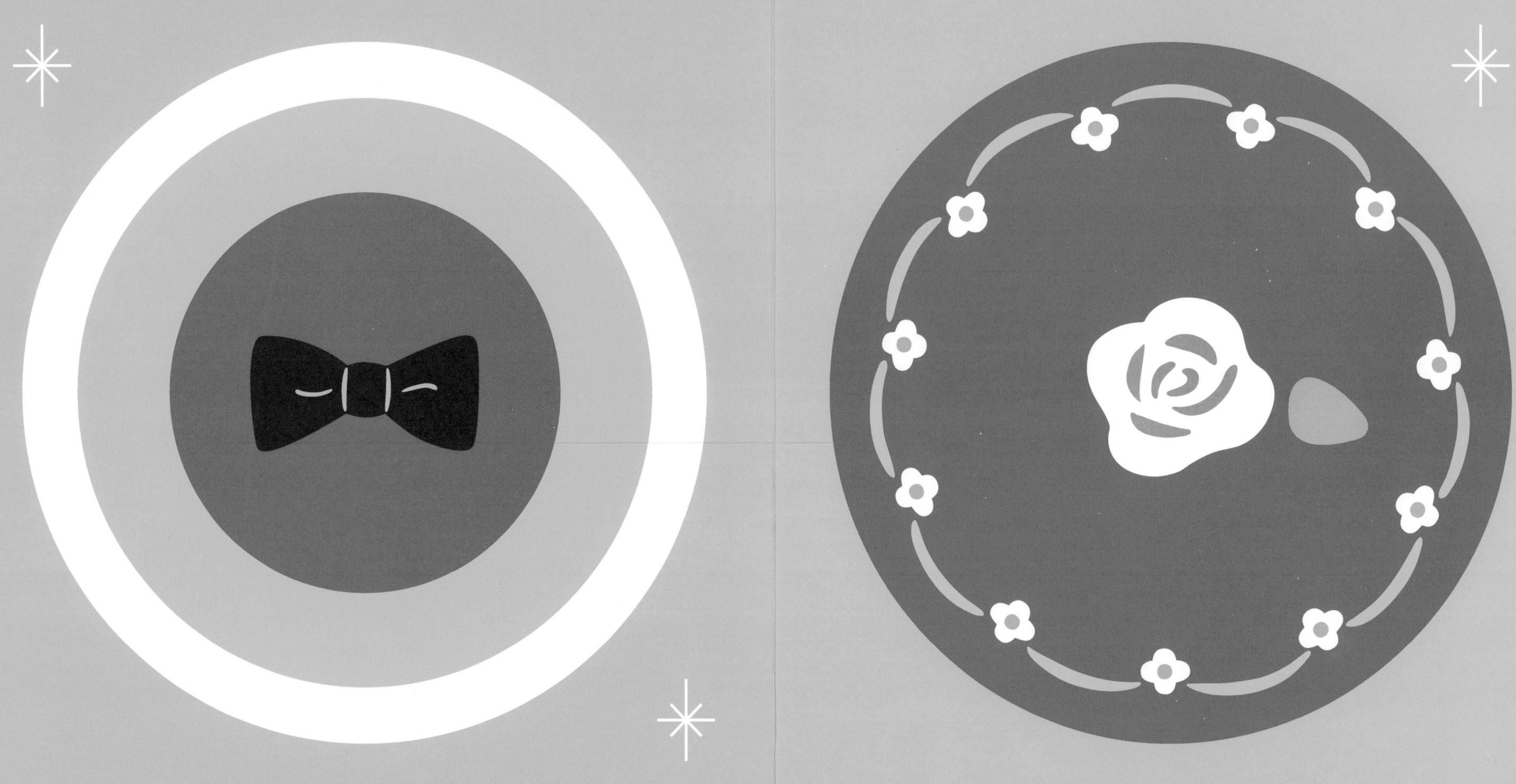